# IMAGES
## OF IRELAND

**Jacket:** *Kilmallock Dominican Abbey*
**Half-title:** *Mount Stewart House and Gardens, Co Down*
**Title page:** *The rugged granite coastline of Connemara at Screeb, Co Galway*
**Contents page:** *The round tower and ruins of St Mary's Augustinian priory on Devenish Island, Co Fermanagh*
**Introduction:** *Looking towards Crookhaven, Co Cork, a favourite place for yachting*

© The Automobile Association 1992
This edition is published by Longmeadow Press, 201 High Ridge Road, Stamford, CT 06904.

Typesetting by Servis Filmsetting Ltd, Manchester
Colour reproduction by Daylight Colour Art Pte Ltd, Singapore
Printed by Proost, b.v. Belgium
Set in Caxton Italic

ISBN 0-681-41818-4

Produced by the Publishing Division of
The Automobile Association

All pictures in this book are taken from
the AA Photographic Library.

Written by Dr Peter Harbison

# IMAGES
## OF IRELAND

LONGMEADOW
PRESS

# CONTENTS

# INTRODUCTION

*I*slands have a fascination. They attract because they offer the sensation of getting away from it all, of reaching somewhere refreshing and faintly exotic far from the humdrum of daily life, and full of people who are the same, yet somehow different. Ireland is such an island.

*A*s islands go, it is comparatively small; during the Ice Age it was joined to Britain, forming a single island larger than the two put together. What the Ice Age left behind when the sea rose was a saucer-like land – flat in the centre and high around the outside, where the finest scenery is found. But it is only the mountains which preserve any glacial memories. The landscape of Ireland today is colourful and clean-aired, with fields separated by hedgerows only a few centuries old, and with cities, towns and villages which provide focal points for cultural and musical activity and, of course, offer opportunities for satisfying the appetite and quenching the thirst.

*T*he 'Four Green Fields of Ireland' make up a land of four happily disparate provinces (and a fifth one of the mind), which bear many traces of mankind's 10,000 years of occupation. Stone Age people buried their dead in imposing megalithic tombs, and in the last millenium before the birth of Christ, the country became increasingly Celtic in its life and language. The Christian era introduced monasteries, which achieved great renown as fosterers of books, metal-work and stone-carving. The Vikings failed to destroy them or their spirit and, instead, contributed to the country's development by founding many of Ireland's larger maritime towns. The Normans, also originally from Scandinavia but coming directly across from Britain, conquered much of the country in the 12th century, and have left a considerable heritage in stone. Planters from Scotland and England, who settled largely in the northern part of Ireland in the 17th century, were the last great body of newcomers to the island.

*A*ll of these have contributed to the lifeblood of an eclectic people who, to this day, have retained a variety of cultural traditions within the country. The Irish are amiable, lively and quixotic, have a way with words, and their sense of humour and hospitality have a quality which instantly breaks down barriers and makes the visitor feel at home.

*I*t is the combination of people, town and landscape that makes Ireland the colourful country illustrated in this book. Set on the periphery of Europe, it is a land where the pace of life moves somewhat slower than at the centre. There is a grain of truth in the old story of the Irishman who, when asked by a Spaniard if the Irish had any word for the concept of *mañana*, replied: 'Yes, señor, there are quite a number. But none of them has quite the same sense of urgency'!

MUNSTER

**Previous page** *The road over Moll's Gap in the glacially denuded hills south-west of Killarney. It was built 150 years ago to encourage traffic from Kenmare at a time when Killarney was becoming one of Ireland's most scenic attractions for early Victorian travellers. History is silent about Moll and why the Gap was named after her.*

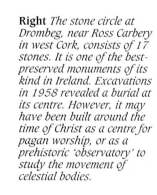

**Right** *The stone circle at Drombeg, near Ross Carbery in west Cork, consists of 17 stones. It is one of the best-preserved monuments of its kind in Ireland. Excavations in 1958 revealed a burial at its centre. However, it may have been built around the time of Christ as a centre for pagan worship, or as a prehistoric 'observatory' to study the movement of celestial bodies.*

**Left** *This beehive-like stone construction houses the mortal remains of one Samuel Grubb, a Quaker. Before he died in the 1920s, he asked to be buried upright on the northern slopes of Sugar Loaf Hill. He chose the site well, for his monument surveys the panoramic plains of south Tipperary. It is located on a road known as The Vee between Clogheen and Lismore.*

**Left** *The beehive huts (round stone houses built without mortar) at Glenfahan have puzzled archaeologists for a century. Were they built by prehistoric shepherds who moved their flocks here seasonally to the Dingle Peninsula? Or were they hostels for pilgrims waiting for good weather to sail to the island of Skellig Michael? Like Chesterton's donkey, they keep their secret still.*

**Below left** *A circular stone house stands within the rampart of a promontory fort at Dunbeg, its back to the ocean and to the Ring of Kerry in the distance. It was probably built about 1,000 years ago. But it may not see much of its second thousand years if Atlantic waves continue to gnaw at the promontory's endangered cliffs.*

**Above left** *The Franciscan friary at Timoleague on the coast of West Cork was founded in 1312 by the dominant local family of Mac Carthy Riabhach, whose burial place it has remained. The friars appear to have survived Henry VIII's Dissolution of the Monasteries in the 1530s, but not the fire inflicted on the friary and the adjacent town in 1642 by an English force under Lord Forbes.*

**Above right** *Kilmallock in Co Limerick was an important town in the Middle Ages, founded by the Anglo-Norman Fitzgeralds. It was they who created its most imposing monument, the Dominican priory, built around 1300. The ruins still preserve delicate traceried windows and fine sculpted details.*

**Right** *Ireland's most dramatic grouping of medieval monuments stands on the Rock of Cashel, which rises abruptly from the plains of Tipperary. Once the seat of the Kings of South Munster, the Rock was given to the Church in 1101. The structures include a round tower, a high cross, a 12th-century stone-roofed church and a 13th-century cathedral. The cathedral was set on fire by the Great Earl of Kildare in 1495 because he 'thought that the archbishop was inside'.*

13

14

**Above** *The sunset glows over the beach at Youghal in east Cork. The town's mayor in 1588–9 was none other than Sir Walter Raleigh. Local tradition fondly believes that he planted Europe's first potatoes there.*

**Right** *The Old Head sticks its nose out into the Atlantic 10 miles (16km) south of Kinsale in Co Cork. It was fortified by a de Courcy castle in the 15th century, and a signal tower was built upon it as a defence against Napoleon. The sinking of the* Lusitania *off the promontory in 1915 helped to bring the United States of America into World War I.*

**Left** *Mizen Head in Co Cork is Ireland's Land's End – the country's most south-westerly point. Its lighthouse is reached by what has been described as 'the most resplendent bridge in Ireland'. At 170ft (52m) the bridge had the largest span reinforced concrete arch in these islands when it was completed in 1910. On clear days, an even more famous lighthouse, the Fastnet Rock, can be seen 10 miles (16km) out to sea.*

15

**Right** *Lough Gur is the only large stretch of water in Co Limerick. Its serene surroundings make it an ideal, if little known, recreational area. The excavation of Ireland's most extensive Stone Age settlement here in the 1930s made Lough Gur into an important archaeological centre.*

**Below** *In Co Kerry roadside flora can include red bouquets of montbretia competing with many other colourful plants. Earlier in the summer, hedgefuls of fuchsia cover the Dingle Peninsula like a hairnet.*

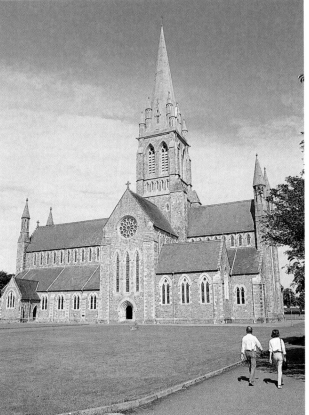

**Opposite** *The romantic 19th-century chapel at Gougane Barra, Co Cork, acts as a focus of tranquillity beside the lake. Near by lay the hermitage of the 6th-century saint, Finbarr, who later moved to Cork. There he founded a monastery where the city now stands. He was later to become his county's favourite saint.*

**Left** *St Mary's Cathedral in Killarney was originally designed in the Neo-Gothic style by the architect AW Pugin (1812–52). Construction work started in 1842, but was interrupted by the Great Famine of 1845–7, some of whose victims it helped to house. The spire was not completed until 1912. In the 1970s, Bishop Eamonn Casey carried out extensive renovations. These included the controversial stripping of Pugin's white plaster from the interior wall surfaces.*

**Below left** *The great Cistercian abbey at Holy Cross in Co Tipperary got its name from a relic of the True Cross which drew many pilgrims to the spot. Its foundation dates back to the 12th century. Considerable reconstruction in the 15th century displays the best of Irish stonemasonry of the period. Careful modern restoration culminated in its re-dedication for Catholic church services in 1975.*

**Left** *From the small west Cork town of Baltimore, travellers can take a ferry to the offshore island of Sherkin. There they can visit the ruins of a Franciscan friary founded by the O'Driscolls in the 15th century, and a research station for marine biology.*

21

**Left** *Today, the town of Baltimore is a haven of peace. Its past history was more troubled, however. In 1577 it was sacked by the men of Waterford in revenge for the seizure of one of their ships. Better known was the raid of Algerian pirates in 1631, which saw 200 of the town's inhabitants carried off to Africa as slaves. The event was commemorated in Thomas Davis's famous ballad,* The Sack of Baltimore.

**Above** *Glandore is one of the many charming harbour villages on the coastline of west Cork. Its history goes back to the 13th century when the Anglo-Norman Barrets built a castle there. It later came into the possession of the O'Donovans.*

22

**Left** *The terraced town of Cobh (pronounced Cove), formerly Queenstown, is dominated by Pugin and Ashlin's Catholic Cathedral of St Colman (1868–1949). It is reputed to have the largest carillon of bells in Ireland. A British naval station until 1937, Cobh was the port of exodus for many of Ireland's 19th-century emigrants. The port witnessed the departure of the* Sirius, *the first steamship to cross the Atlantic successfully (1838), as well as its luckless successor, the* Titanic *(1912).*

**Above** *A contrast to Cobh is provided by the quiet west Clare town of Milltown Malbay, home of Ireland's former President, Dr Patrick Hillery. Its colourful streetscape reflects the fact that many of the smaller Irish towns only came into being during the mid-Victorian era.*

24

**Right** *Schull is one of the best-known holiday villages of Co Cork. In the midday sun, the younger generation relax here on benches outside a restaurant named in Irish 'The Little House'.*

**Left** *The market-place of Macroom is dominated by the remnants of a castle which Cromwell gave to Admiral Sir William Penn, father of William Penn, the founder of Pennsylvania. Here in 1768 Eileen Dubh O'Connell met and fell in love with Art O'Leary, in whose memory she wrote one of the most famous Gaelic poems of the time.*

**Below** *The pavement on Cork city's main thoroughfare, St Patrick Street, is broad enough for the artist to complete his colourful masterpiece. There, he will hope to gain more than just approving glances from the interested passers-by.*

25

**Above** *The Blue Haven Hotel in Kinsale is a renowned example of the small family-run hotel which provides comfortable accommodation and high-quality Irish cuisine. With its numerous hotels and restaurants, Kinsale has built up the reputation of being Ireland's gastronomic capital.*

**Above** *The tastefully designed lettering above the door and the projecting pub sign invite the visitor to food and drink at Furey's in Macroom, Co Cork. Further advertisements for products past and present add to the décor and titillate the senses.*

**Above** *Pubs are an institution in rural Ireland. Few have such a strong visual appeal as Dan Foley's in Anascaul, Co Kerry. The vivid colours of its exterior give a foretaste of the lively conversation and the magic within. Dan, formerly a circus magician, often entertains his customers.*

**Above** *Muckross House in Killarney was built in 1843 by H A Herbert, MP for Kerry from 1847 to 1866. Queen Victoria was his guest here in 1861. In 1932, the house was presented to the nation by its American owners, the Bourns and the Vincents. Within, the mansion is furnished largely in Victorian style, but it is also a Museum of Kerry Folk Life, and has workshops actively producing a variety of modern crafts.*

**Left** *Jarveys in Killarney town offer horse-drawn tours to the Muckross Estate and Bourn-Vincent National Park. They waft the modern tourist back to the halcyon days of one-horse power enjoyed by our ancestors.*

**Above** *From the peaceful water near Moll's Gap, the road winds down towards Killarney. There, some of Ireland's most sublime scenery awaits the traveller around the shores of the famous lakes.*

**Right** *On the road from Kenmare, a stop at Ladies View provides the first glimpse of Killarney and gives some hint of the scenic delights that lie ahead. The barrenness of the surrounding hills gradually gives way to the gentle, wooded slopes which have made Killarney a byword for beauty.*

**Above** *The quickest way of moving around the Muckross Estate in Killarney is in an open jaunting car. Automobiles are not permitted. The grandeur of the scenery drew from the celebrated 18th-century Bishop Berkeley the comment, 'another Louis Quatorze may make another Versailles, but the hand of the Deity only can make another Muckross'.*

30

**Right** *The Connor Pass, on the Tralee to Dingle road, offers the opportunity of seeing the remains of a barren Ice Age landscape. Small plants cling to the hillsides scraped of vegetation by retreating glaciers, which left small lakes behind them as they melted.*

**Below** *Fine woodland is found in the National Park at Gougane Barra. Opened to the public in 1966, the Park offers sylvan walks for the recreation seeker. Here, too, is the source of the river which Corkmen proudly sing of in their County Anthem, 'On the Banks of my own lovely Lee'.*

32

**Right** *'The Golden Vale' aptly describes the rich farmlands in the plains of Tipperary. Characteristic are the isolated farmsteads and the hedgerows, which stitch together a patchwork of fields and give wildlife some cover. The hedgerows have, however, been in place only a few centuries. Formerly, the Irish countryside was much more heavily wooded.*

**Above** *Irish roads are for more than the motor car. With not too much traffic on the smaller roads, a walk or hike is a pleasant experience. It gives more time to enjoy a landscape, such as that looking towards Allihies in west Cork.*

**Top** *In the south and west of Ireland particularly, donkeys provide a delightful, if unexpected, addition to the Irish menagerie. Originally beasts of burden useful in craggy terrain, they can still occasionally be seen bringing milk to the rural creamery. But, more often than not, they are now just kept as pets.*

**Above right** *A French writer once remarked that Irish cattle showed a preference for the grass in the middle of the road. They are also known to cause bemused traffic jams around milking time. But here, at Slea Head, they have a car-less passage.*

**Right** *Blarney Castle rises 85ft (26m) above a rock some five miles (8km) north-west of Cork city. One of the most imposing of the country's medieval tower-houses, it was built by Cormac Láidir (The Strong) Mac Carthy in 1446. His family lost it to the Jefferyes in the Williamite confiscations at the end of the 17th century. Later it passed to the Colthursts, who remain the private owners today. Their 19th-century stately home in the castle grounds is also open to the public.*

**Below** *Blarney is synonymous with flowery talk. Just below its castle's battlements is the 'Blarney Stone'. In the words of Father Prout,*
*'A stone that whoever kisses O, he never misses to grow eloquent'.*
*Few Irish think that they need to have recourse to it, but others flock to Blarney to lie on their back and kiss the underside of the stone. It has given rise to many a story about its origin – but which one to believe?*

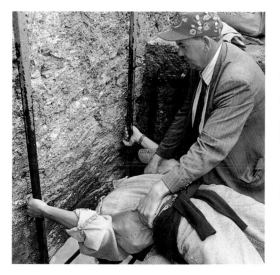

**Above** *The tall, round donjon at Nenagh in Co Tipperary is part of a powerful castle built in the early 13th century by the Anglo-Norman Theobald Walter, a nephew of St Thomas à Becket. The castle changed ownership many times before a farmer blew up part of the wall around 1760 to get rid of sparrows which were ruining his crops. The windows on top are a 19th-century addition.*

**Above right** *Kanturk Castle in north Cork is a mixture of late medieval Irish tower-house and Tudor mansion. Construction was started by Dermod Mac Owen Mac Donagh around 1601. It was never finished, either because the Battle of Kinsale put an end to his affluence, or because he could borrow no more money to complete it.*

**Right** *Reginald's Tower on Waterford's Quays takes its name from Ragnvald the Dane, who is said to have built it in 1003. The tower, however, is much more likely to have been constructed at a much later period. It was allegedly in an upper floor of the tower that the Norman knight, Strongbow, married Aoife, daughter of the king of Leinster, in 1170. This event was to change the course of Irish history. Some of that history is on display within the tower.*

39

**Above** *Lismore Castle in Co Waterford looks like a palace in a fairy tale. Prince John first fortified the site in 1185, but much of the present structure dates from the mid-19th century. It was designed for the 6th Duke of Devonshire by Joseph Paxton, best known as the architect of the Crystal Palace. The gardens are open to the public, but not the castle itself.*

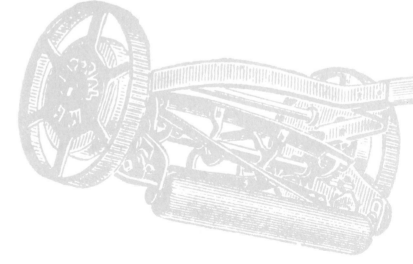

**Above left** *Smaller Irish towns and villages are usually well kept. At least in high summer, anyway, when the judges come around in the annual Tidy Towns Competition, organised by the Irish Tourist Board. Sneem, in Co Kerry, was the outright winner in 1987.*

**Left** *An overworked signpost pole at Timoleague, Co Cork, with the place-names in Irish and English. In accordance with EC usage, distances are normally stated in kilometres. Older finger posts on minor roads, however, frequently retain the distance in miles.*

**Above** *Watching the world go by. Brightly painted façades and the occasional mural enliven many a street in Ireland. The artist of this trompe l'oeil in Ross Carbery, west Cork, obviously didn't take life too seriously.*

42

**Left** *Crookhaven is a well-sheltered cruising ground for sailors, young and old. Those who want to 'potter around in boats' can do so to their heart's content along the varied coastline of west Cork.*

**Opposite** *Dunmanus Bay, Co Cork, divides two of the five peninsulas which project, like fingers, out into the Atlantic on the south-west coast of Ireland. The views they offer are rarely less than memorable and often more than stunning.*

43

**Left** *Seals bask in the sunshine on a small islet in Glengarriff harbour. The Gulf Stream gives the south-west of Ireland a warm climate and an almost sub-tropical vegetation.*

**Above** *Kinsale is perhaps the most charming and outward-looking of all the smaller Irish ports. Irish hopes of independence were twice dashed there. The first time was in 1601 when the forces of Queen Elizabeth I defeated a fleet arriving with help from Spain. The second was in 1690, when the Stewart King James II finally departed for France after his unsuccessful stand against William of Orange.*

**Right** *Schull harbour is a favourite mooring for yachtsmen sailing the waters of west Cork. As in many another harbour along the coast, they will usually find more than water to drink when they go ashore.*

47

**Left** *The circular tour around the Iveragh Peninsula is known as 'The Ring of Kerry'. It rewards the motorist with a constantly varying interplay of hill and cloud. There, too, the roadside botanist will find much to please and excite.*

**Above** *Rich foliage adorns the thatched cottages at Adare in Co Limerick. Their orderly layout is reminiscent of the west of England. The whole village owes its exotic appearance to Edwin, the 3rd Earl of Dunraven (1812–71), an Oxford Movement convert to Catholicism. He was one of the best 'improving landlords' of his day.*

**Left** *Bantry House was built for Richard White, 1st Earl of Bantry, in the mid-18th century. Beautifully located beside Bantry Bay, it is still owned by his descendants, the Shelswell-Whites. The period furnishings include some owned by Marie-Antoinette. It is west Cork's premier stately home open to the public.*

**Above left** *Ilnacullin (Garinish Island) near Glengarriff in Bantry Bay has the finest garden in the south-west of Ireland. The barren island was bought by Belfast-born MP Annan Bryce in 1910. He employed the English architect and garden designer, Harold Peto, to transform it into a magical Italianate garden. Carefully maintained by the State since 1953, it is reachable by a frequent boat service from the nearby mainland. It is open daily from March till October.*

**Above** *Adare Manor in Co Limerick was erected from 1831 onwards by the 2nd Earl of Dunraven (1782–1850). Much of the design was his own work, but for some of the details he employed architects like Hardwick and Pugin. No longer a family residence, it now receives guests and plays host to an international music festival in the month of July.*

**Above** *In Carrick-on-Suir in Co Tipperary stands Ireland's finest surviving mansion of the Tudor period. It was built by 'Black Tom' Butler, the 10th Earl of Ormond, as an addition to a taller 15th-century tower. The mansion contains stucco portraits of Queen Elizabeth I. Her mother, Anne Boleyn, a granddaughter of the 7th Earl, is traditionally said to have been born here.*

**Right** *King John's Castle in Limerick was built in the early years of the 13th century. The site had previously been occupied and defended by both Norse and native Irish. An interpretive centre, built within the castle's walls in 1991, tells the history of the city and its fortification.*

**Left** *Bunratty Castle was built in the mid-15th century by the MacConmara family. A hundred years later it was in the hands of the O'Briens, Earls of Thomond. It now houses furnishings of the later Middle Ages and is the scene of nightly medieval-style banquets. Adjoining the castle is a folk park displaying thatched houses of the last century, as well as a reconstructed Victorian village.*

**Left** *Beautifully located on the Shannon estuary, Glin Castle was built around 1770 and castellated half a century later. It is the home of Desmond Fitzgerald, the Knight of Glin, and his family, who are descended from the Norman Geraldines, occupants of the area for about 700 years. The castle may be viewed by appointment.*

**Above** *For all its ruggedness the mountain scenery of the south-west of Ireland often beckons to the motorist with a smile. Here, the Glengarriff-Kenmare road links the counties of Cork and Kerry.*

**Above right** *A Calvary group casts an evening shadow over the Healy Pass, 1,084ft (330m), which crosses the mountainous Beara Peninsula in west Cork. The name commemorates local statesman T M Healy (1885–1931), leader of the Irish Party at Westminster and first Governor-General of the Irish Free State.*

**Right** *A wayside shrine in honour of the Blessed Virgin Mary. Her cult was given a great boost in Ireland by the Marian Year of 1954, which inspired a host of grottoes throughout the country.*

**Right** *A gleaming white beacon stands high, overlooking Baltimore Bay in west Cork, as a landmark for yachtsmen. The area plays host to the successful Glenans sailing school.*

**Right** *From the southern side of the Dingle Peninsula in Co Kerry, Inch strand stretches oceanwards as one long and lovely sandbank. It is safe for bathers and is much beloved of horse- and pony-riders.*

**Left** *The village of Waterville is a convenient stop halfway around the Ring of Kerry. Guarding the entrance to Lough Currane, it is not only an important centre for the trout-fisher, but also for the golfer.*

**Above** *Like a layered cake, the Cliffs of Moher rise 688ft (210m) above the Atlantic waves on the west coast of Co Clare. O'Brien's Tower was erected near the edge of the precipice in 1835.*

**Right** *The sugar-beet growers of Courtmacsherry in Co Cork seem to get their sweet revenge by showing a healthy disregard for local authority.*

56

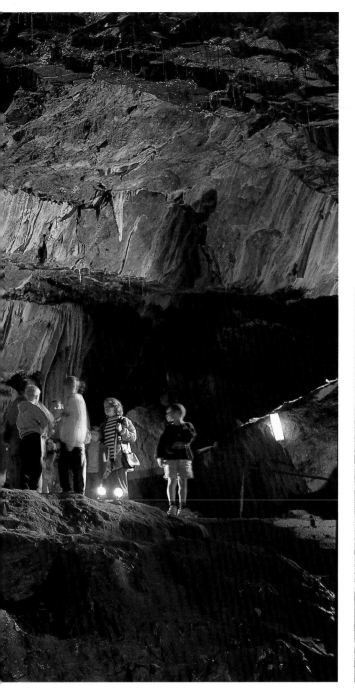

57

**Above** *Mitchelstown Caves, near Ballyporeen in Co Tipperary, are reputed to have the largest cave chamber in Britain and Ireland. They were the hiding place of the tragic Sugán Earl of Desmond, who was betrayed by his kinsman, the White Knight, in 1601. A whole new part of the cave was discovered in 1833.*

**Above** *Tunnel vision. Engineers linking Glengarriff to Kenmare in the last century found it easier to carve the road out of the hillside than to build a way around it.*

**Above** *Passage East is a tidy fishing hamlet on the western shore of Waterford Harbour. A ferry from here brings cars across the estuary to Arthurstown and Ballyhack. The village saw the arrival of the Norman conqueror, Strongbow, on his way to capture Waterford in 1170, followed the next year by King Henry II with 4,000 men in 400 ships.*

**Left** *Dunquin at the end of the Dingle Peninsula in Co Kerry is known as 'the next parish to America'. It is still one of the bastions of the Irish language. The inhabitants of the offshore Blasket Islands used to come here to shop and bury their dead. They finally came to settle here when the islands were abandoned in 1953.*

**Right** *Glenbeigh, Co Kerry, has re-created a bog village of the kind used in the area for the last few hundred years. The simple cottages were sometimes single-roomed. They were thatched and would have had a yearly coat of whitewash. Hay machines, milk churns and turf, as a welcome fuel, were part of the rural life of earlier generations.*

**Below** *Ballybunion in north-west Kerry has a championship golf course overlooking the Atlantic. Proximity to the sea provides links courses with sand dunes. Their undulations offer the player plenty of variety – and maram grass to trap the errant golf ball. Most of the new courses currently being developed in Ireland are, however, inland.*

**Left** *Across the sound from Dunquin in west Kerry lie the Blasket Islands. Totally Irish-speaking until they left some 40 years ago, the islands' inhabitants were famed for the beauty of their almost Homeric language and literature. Three books which emanated from the only village on the Great Blasket became internationally famous when translated into English and other languages.*

**Above** *A farmer in Co Limerick might seem to be in danger of overwatering the plants in his yard. But his pump is probably dry, and he is more likely now to get his $H_2O$ supplied through a community piped water scheme.*

63

**Overleaf** *The coastline west of Dingle is heavily indented. According to the medieval tale known as* The Battle of Ventry, *it was here that the legendary hero Finn Mac Cumhaill overcame the man who was emperor of the whole world except Ireland!*

LEINSTER

**Previous page** *Tacumshane Windmill in Co Wexford was built by the millwright Nicholas Moran in 1846, and ground exceeding well for 90 years. Reconstruction of the machinery in 1952 enabled it to remain one of the last Irish windmills to survive intact. But the sails, once turned by gentle offshore winds, now no longer whirr around, awaiting a Don Quixote to challenge them into life again.*

**Right** *Tully House on the outskirts of Kildare town is the home of Ireland's National Stud. It was founded in 1902 by Colonel William Hill-Walker, later Lord Wavertree, and is now owned and administered by the Irish government. The stud provides expert advice to the Irish bloodstock industry, and is also a centre for research in thoroughbred breeding.*

**Below** *The National Stud has a high reputation for the foals it produces, which command good prices at the bloodstock sales at home and abroad. In a museum in the grounds is the skeleton of Arkle, one of the most famous of all steeplechasers.*

**Above left** *Avondale House, near Rathdrum in Co Wicklow, is now a museum commemorating Charles Stewart Parnell (1846–91), whose home it was. As leader of the Irish Party at Westminster, Parnell almost succeeded in obtaining Home Rule for Ireland, but a celebrated divorce case in 1890 brought his aspirations to a premature end and hastened his own early death.*

**Above** *The pebble-paved terrace of Powerscourt House in Co Wicklow leads to the stepped gardens and their vista of the Great Sugarloaf Mountain (1,654ft/504m). The gardens were laid out (1843–75) by Daniel Robertson. The story goes that he did his designing while being wheeled around in a barrow, holding a bottle of sherry. When the sherry ran out, he stopped work till the following day.*

**Above** *The monastery at Clonmacnois in Co Offaly was founded close to the River Shannon by St Ciarán around 545. It still exudes a feeling of great peace and calm. A noted centre of the arts 1,000 years ago, it boasts many churches, crosses and two round towers.*

**Right** *The Stone Age burial mound at Newgrange in the Boyne Valley is one of the world's first great pieces of architecture. Built around 3100BC, it may be 500 years older than the Pyramids. The wall-facing of white quartzite is modern.*

**Below** *The dolmen in Browne's Hill Demesne, near Carlow town, is one of the most impressive examples of its kind in Ireland. Its capstone is reputed to weigh 100 tons – no wonder one end has fallen to the ground. It was built as a tomb during the Stone Age, some 5,000 years ago.*

**Bottom** *The entrance stone to the passage tomb at Newgrange is one of Europe's noblest prehistoric carvings. Its spiral and lozenge designs had a symbolism now beyond our ken. The modern walling behind it surrounds the entrance to the tomb.*

**Above** *Muiredach's Cross at Monasterboice, Co Louth, was probably erected around the middle of the 9th century. One of its many carved panels shows Christ in his purple robe and bearing a reed. He is being mocked by the Roman soldiers as they hailed him as 'King of the Jews'.*

**Above right** *The head of the market cross in Kells, Co Meath, shows the crucified Christ at the centre of a ring, probably conceived as a cosmic symbol. Kells was for long the home of the Book of Kells, the great illuminated manuscript now in the library of Trinity College, Dublin.*

**Right** *The 100ft (30m) round tower dominates the ancient monastery of Glendalough, deep in the Wicklow Hills. Some think these towers were erected as bastions against the marauding Vikings, but they may have been designed as beacons to guide pilgrims to the hallowed site.*

**Opposite** *Outlined against the rising sun is the 14th-century tower of St Mary's Augustinian abbey in Trim, Co Meath. A statue of the Virgin, known as 'The Idol of Trim', was venerated here during the Middle Ages. The town of Trim has many other interesting medieval ruins.*

76

**Above** *Guinness's brewery preserves wooden barrels in which its stout was transported in years gone by. They have now been replaced by metal casks. This famous Dublin brewery was founded by Arthur Guinness in 1759, but its headquarters have now moved to London.*

**Right** *Locke's distillery in Kilbeggan, Co Westmeath, produced a mellow whiskey in its heyday, but has long since ceased to function, alas. However, the buildings and machinery have been restored as a museum in recent years. Irish whiskey is always spelled with an e.*

**Above** *'The butcher, the baker, the candlestickmaker' runs the old rhyme. Not candlesticks but their contents are made at Rathborne's on Dublin's East Wall Road. One of the oldest surviving practitioners of the chandler's trade, they recently commemorated their first 500 years in the business.*

**Left** *A bookbinder uses traditional methods as he practises his craft in the studios at Marlay Park, Rathfarnham, in the foothills of the Dublin Mountains. In the 18th century Dublin was renowned for its classical morocco bookbindings.*

**Above right** *Colm Maher, a traditional Irish harp maker, tunes a new instrument made in the workshops at Marlay Park, a hive of many craft activities. The country's symbol, the harp is emblazoned on Ireland's coat of arms.*

**Above** *The village of Ballitore in Co Kildare proudly preserves a mill and other mementoes of its industrious Quaker past. Abraham Shackleton (1697–1771) came from Yorkshire to found a Quaker school here. Among its pupils was Edmund Burke, later to become an illustrious orator.*

**Above right** *The Irish National Heritage Park at Ferrycarrig, near Wexford town, brings the Irish past to life. It has reconstructions of various aspects of old Irish life. One is a crannóg, or artificial island, of a kind used by the Irish to defend themselves more than 1,000 years ago.*

**Right** *Silk painting painstakingly executed in the Tower Enterprise Centre in Dublin. This is one of the more prominent workshops in the nation's capital where younger talent can practise its various crafts and sell them to an appreciative public.*

**Left** *Powerscourt House Shopping Centre quickly became a focus for chic shoppers when it opened in the 1980s. Once the open-air back yard of one of Dublin's most elegant town houses, it has proved to be a most successful conversion. It offers colour and fashion, often with live piano accompaniment.*

**Top** *Crowds are always bustling around Easons, Dublin's largest stationer-cum-bookshop. It is centrally located on O'Connell Street, named after the popular statesman Daniel O'Connell (1775–1847). Spaciously laid out in the 18th century, this is the capital's widest shopping street.*

**Above** *The old-fashioned narrow streets of Wexford offer plenty to look at in the shop windows. The town is particularly lively in the Hallowe'en period when it mounts one of the most enjoyable of Europe's smaller opera festivals. Everyone joins in the fun.*

**Above left** *The Dubliner is very attached to his pub. At Foley's in Merrion Row, for instance, he can get a liquid lunch. He may also be seen retiring there after work to consort with his friends over a good pint of whatever takes his fancy.*

**Left** *Leaning on his stick, the bronze James Joyce surveys the modern Dublin scene from his pedestal in Talbot Street. The statue is one of the city's gestures to honour the man whose description of Dublin in his novel* Ulysses *is now a world classic.*

**Above** *The Cultúrlann (Irish for house or hall of culture) in Dublin's suburb of Monkstown offers concerts of traditional Irish music. Some of the most talented fiddlers and other instrumentalists gather here to delight audiences with their playing.*

**Above right** *As in London, Dublin's Fleet Street is a hub of press activity. In the Palace Bar there, Bertie Smyllie, genial editor of* The Irish Times, *was the central figure of a galaxy of budding and well-established literati during the 1930s and 1940s.*

*Theatre poster advertises a play adapted from a book by the Irish comic author, Flann O'Brien. Plays by Lady Gregory and W B Yeats (who together founded the theatre in 1904), Synge and O'Casey made the Abbey world famous. The present building dates from 1966.*

**Left** *Eighteenth-century Dublin was, and still is, an elegant city. Its houses, built with warm red brick, are entered through doorways with classically inspired fanlights. Originally family town houses, their brass plates now bear the names of doctors and solicitors.*

**Above** *Not everything you see on a Dublin Georgian doorway belongs to the 18th century. Careful examination can bring later details to light, as revealed by the decorative style of lettering on this more recent letter box.*

**Opposite bottom** *The brightly painted doorways of Dublin's Georgian houses follow classical lines. Yet few are ever exactly the same, and the door-spotter will have endless fun studying their permutations and combinations.*

**Left** *Christ Church Cathedral is Dublin's oldest surviving place of religious worship. It was founded by a Christian Norse king of the city in 1038. Part of the structure goes back to the 12th century, but many of its present furnishings are the result of an extensive 19th-century restoration.*

**Above** *St Michan's Protestant church is on the site of Dublin's first Norse church north of the River Liffey. Its fine organ, of around 1725, bears a wooden panel of musical instruments probably carved by John Houghton.*

**Overleaf** *The Throne Room in Dublin Castle was re-modelled by the architect Francis Johnston in the later 18th century. The oval painted panels are probably by a Venetian artist. Dublin Castle was the centre of British power in Ireland from about 1200 until 1922. Its classical interiors have recently been restored to their original splendour.*

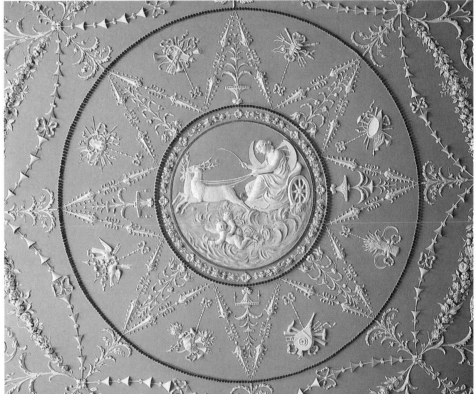

**Left** *Abbeyleix House in Co Laois has been the home of the De Vesci family for two and a half centuries. The design is variously attributed to Sir William Chambers or James Wyatt. Built in the middle of the 18th century, the house is surrounded by fine gardens, but neither is open to the public.*

**Top** *The Chinese ceiling in the Chester Beatty Library and Gallery of Oriental Art, in Shrewsbury Road, Dublin. This all-too-little-known gem of a library and gallery houses one of the western world's finest collections of Islamic and Far Eastern manuscripts, bindings and other artefacts. It was presented to the Irish nation on the death of the American mining engineer, Sir Alfred Chester Beatty, in 1968.*

**Above** *This plasterwork ceiling, featuring Diana the huntress, is one of the glories of Belvedere House in Great Denmark Street, Dublin. Its artist, Michael Stapleton, was a stuccodore in the Adamesque style who built the house around 1785 for William Rochfort, 2nd Earl of Belvedere. Since 1841, the house has been a Jesuit school, once attended by James Joyce.*

93

94

**Left** *The Palm House in the National Botanic Gardens in the Dublin suburb of Glasnevin luxuriates with tropical greenery. The Gardens were founded in 1795 by the Royal Dublin Society and taken over by the State in 1878. One of its conservatories is by Richard Turner, who designed another for Kew Gardens.*

**Above** *Golden vine leaves decorate the ornamental iron gates at the entrance to the garden of Powerscourt Estate in Co Wicklow. The gates are said to have been brought here from Bamberg in Bavaria, but are probably Viennese in origin.*

**Above** *The Japanese Gardens on the outskirts of Kildare town were created by Lord Wavertree. He hired the Japanese gardener Eida and his son Minora to design them between 1906 and 1910. They trace symbolically the Path of Life from the Cave of Birth, and thence through various vicissitudes to the Garden of Peace and Contentment.*

95

**Right** *The Royal Dublin Society's Horse Show in August is one of the most important events in Dublin's social life. The Society was founded in 1731 to promote the application of practical economics, and has ever since been an enthusiastic supporter of agriculture, the sciences and the arts. Another of its significant events is the Spring Show, which displays the best of the country's agricultural and industrial products.*

**Right, and above left**
*Dublin's Zoological Gardens were founded in 1830. They are located in Phoenix Park in the north-western sector of Dublin city. Here, a wide variety of animals, birds and reptiles may be viewed at leisure in pleasantly wooded surroundings. The zoo has had considerable success over the years in breeding lions in captivity. The feeding of the seals in the afternoon invariably draws crowds of children, who flock to the zoo for a combination of education and entertainment.*

97

**Left** *Earlier generations of Irishmen were not great fish-eaters. But from the catches of fishing boats like these in Balbriggan Harbour, north of Dublin, they learned to savour the delights of fresh herring, mackerel, plaice, lobster and other* fruits de mer.

**Top** *Canoeing is a colourful sport for the young and for those who remain young at heart. Canoes have the advantage that they can be paddled not only on inland waters, but also on the sea – as here at the family holiday resort of Courtown Harbour, Co Wexford.*

**Above** *In the peace of the early morning, while the rest of the world is still fast asleep, the fisherfolk of Skerries, Co Dublin, go out in their boats in the hope of filling their nets. That same evening, some of the day's fresh haul is served up – suitably garnished, of course – in the town's fish restaurant, 'The Red Bank'.*

**Right** *Having found a foothold on the weir slope at Slane, Co Meath, a lone fisherman tries his luck, close to where the famous Battle of the Boyne was fought in 1690. The Boyne has always been famed as a salmon river.*

**Above** *The architect James Wyatt designed Slane Castle for William Burton Conyngham, a noted art patron, in 1786. It was here that George IV came in 1821 to visit his mistress, Elizabeth, Marchioness Conyngham, though some of his beautiful gifts to her were damaged in a fire in 1991. The biggest rock concerts ever seen in Ireland were staged in the large field in front of the castle – promoted by its present owner, Lord Henry Mount Charles.*

102

**Left** *The library of Trinity College, Dublin, was designed by Thomas Burgh (1712–32) with two superimposed storeys. However, by removing part of the floor in between and adding a vaulted ceiling in 1860, Benjamin Woodward magically transformed it into one of the most majestic architectural spaces in Ireland. The library houses the Book of Kells, the Book of Durrow and many other treasures of the college.*

**Above** *The grounds of Trinity College are like an oasis of fresh air in the centre of Dublin. The college shows its back to the city and faces inwards on to its own green lung. Twins externally, the College Chapel (left) and the Theatre or Examination Hall (in shadow on the right), designed by Sir William Chambers and Graham Myers in the 1780s, eye one another across the cobblestones of Front Square. The lofty campanile of 1853 is said to mark the site of the monastery of All Hallows, upon which Trinity College was first built in 1592.*

104

**Right** *In front of the National Gallery of Ireland, on the west side of Dublin's Merrion Square, stands a statue of the railway magnate, William Dargan (1799–1867). It was funds for a testimonial in his honour that helped to create the Gallery, which has a good representative collection from most of the important schools of European painting. George Bernard Shaw left a third of his estate to the Gallery, in gratitude for which his statue was also placed in the grounds.*

THE RIGHT HON. THEOPHILUS LORD NEWTOWN OF NEWTOWN BUTLER BEQUEATH° TO THE POOR OF ST. ANNS PARISH FOR EVER THIRTEEN POUNDS PER ANNUM TO BE DISTRIBUTED IN BREAD AT FIVE SHILLINGS EACH WEEK
1723

**Top** *The dining hall of Trinity College dates back to a design by Richard Cassels (1745–9) and is still in daily use by the students. When a fire threatened the splendid interior in 1984, teaching staff heroically rescued most of its contents, including an over-life-size portrait of George IV as Prince of Wales.*

**Above** *Five shillings' worth of bread per week would keep precious few poor people alive today. But it must have seemed a princely benefaction when bequeathed by Lord Newton in 1723 to the poor of St Ann's parish. To this day, bread is still placed on shelves on either side of the chancel in St Ann's Church, in Dublin's fashionable Dawson Street.*

106

**Above** *Not a pig escaping from the kitchen, but the Erymanthine Boar illustrating one of the Labours of Hercules on the stairway of Ely House, Dublin. The interior decoration of the house was as lavish as the extravagance of its builder, Henry Loftus, later Earl of Ely, could afford. Designed in 1770 by Michael Stapleton, the house is now owned by the Knights of Columbanus.*

**Right** *Many a masterpiece was created by Irish craftsmen in the decoration of 18th-century houses. This one ornaments a door in Fitzwilliam Square, an elegant product of late-Georgian Dublin.*

**Below** *The Olympia is one of Dublin's oldest theatres. Originally the Empire Palace of Varieties, and later Dan Lowry's Music Hall, the theatre now offers a wide variety of musical and dramatic entertainment in its colourful interior. To the delight of its patrons, the bars remain open after the fall of the curtain.*

**Above** *The statue of Daniel O'Connell (1775–1847) dominates one end of Dublin's widest thoroughfare, which is now named after him. The figure of O'Connell is largely the work of the Dublin sculptor John Henry Foley (1818–74), who is also known for his contribution to the Albert Memorial in London. The committee which oversaw the completion of the monument met 214 times over a period of 20 years. A record?*

**Right** *The O'Connell Street fountain presented to Dublin city in celebration of its millennium year in 1988 has as its focal point a recumbent statue of Anna Livia, the embodiment of the River Liffey. As the poet Brendan Kennelly says, 'Dubliners love to hate her'. They have their own irreverent nicknames for her – the floozie in the jacuzzi, the bitch in the ditch, the bride in the tide, and the whore (pronounced 'huer') in the sewer!*

**Left** *Many Dublin lamp standards, like this one in O'Connell Street, bear the city's coat of arms. The motto* Obedientia civium urbis felicitas *may be roughly rendered as 'Happy the city where citizens obey'.*

**Above** *Old traditions die hard. The horse and the cart, with modern car wheels and rubber tyres, is a reminder of how grandfather would have had his food and fuel delivered in the Dublin suburbs. Until recently, one could occasionally catch sight of crushed motor cars being ignominiously carried through the streets on a cart like this.*

**Left** *Except for one brief interlude, Malahide Castle, eight miles (13km) from the centre of Dublin, was owned by the Talbot family from the 12th century until 1973. Subsequently bought by Dublin County Council, the castle is now open to the public, who can inspect most of the family furniture and portraits, along with the National Portrait Gallery. The castle grounds are particularly attractive.*

**Left** *In the 1890s, Lever Brothers built Sunlight Chambers on the corner of Parliament Street and Essex Quay, overlooking the River Liffey. The building's terracotta friezes seem to illustrate industrious Victorian virtues in mock-Renaissance style. Anticipating TV ads, these water-bearing washerwomen obviously bear witness to the advantages of laundering with Lever Brothers' super Sunlight soap.*

**Left** *The Parsons family, Earls of Rosse, have been in possession of Birr Castle, Co Offaly, since 1620, and they enlarged it to its present size after a fire in 1823. In the grounds is the case of a telescope, which was the largest in the world when built by the 3rd Earl (1800–67), an astronomer who discovered the spiral nebulae. His nephew, Charles, invented the steam turbine. Visitors are welcomed in the gardens and the tea-house on the estate.*

**Above** *Is the wink as good as a nod? Not if you are trying to discover whose is this face on the outside of the Iveagh Market in Dublin's Francis Street. As one of eight stone heads, some say it represents one of the eight races of mankind. Others say it represents the Earl of Iveagh, a public benefactor who gave many things to the capital city, including this market built in 1906.*

CONNACHT

**Previous page** *The two Yeats brothers, WB the poet and JB the painter, spent their childhood summers close to what they called 'Memory Harbour'. Here, at Rosses Point in Co Sligo, there is now a championship golf course, two beaches and – not altogether surprisingly – a yacht club. The name Yeats is now indelibly associated with the beautiful landscape of Co Sligo.*

**Above** *Galway is the largest and most important town in Connacht. Its hub is Eyre Square, a relaxing meeting place for city folk and tourists alike, and the gateway to Connemara and the Aran Islands.*

**Above** *Knock in Co Mayo is one of the most significant places of pilgrimage in Ireland. It was on the gable of the old church there that the Virgin Mary and other figures are alleged to have appeared in 1879. Pope John Paul II visited Knock in its centenary year, and Monsignor Horan, the parish priest, inspired the building of a large airport near by to bring in pilgrims from Britain and America.*

**Left** *Ballina is the largest town in Co Mayo. It is beloved of fishermen, as it stands at the mouth of one of the country's best salmon rivers, the Moy. But recently Ballina has, perhaps, become best known as the home town of Ireland's popular President, Mrs Mary Robinson.*

**Below** *Salthill is a seaside resort, and the recreational playground for Galway city. There is all the fun of the fair in summer, with plenty of entertainment, either organised or of your own making.*

*119*

**Above** *Bungalows may have become the desirable residences of modern Ireland. But the traditional thatched house is much more picturesque in the Connemara countryside. No matter how humble, it fits snugly as a fresh mushroom in any Irish landscape.*

**Above** *In the granite terrain of Connemara, as in many other parts of rural Ireland, there is sometimes a superstitious reluctance to demolish old dwellings. Here, in Roundstone, re-roofing part of the ruin has given it a new lease of life and adds what might seem like rust-ic charm.*

**Above** *The ruined Cistercian abbey at Boyle, Co Roscommon, stands obligingly adjacent to the Dublin–Sligo road. Medieval annals written here, and now preserved in the British Library in London, indicate a foundation date of 1161. The buildings, however, were constructed over a long period in changing architectural styles. After the Dissolution of the Monasteries by Henry VIII, the monks' living quarters served as a barracks and hence suffered considerable damage in the Cromwellian wars.*

**Right** *The granite boulder at Turoe, not far from Loughrea, Co Galway, is a rare Irish example of a decorated Iron Age stone, which may be a copy of a wooden original. Its typically Celtic curvilinear ornament suggests a date in the last few centuries BC. But only imagination can assist us in envisaging what its druidic ritual or cult role may once have been.*

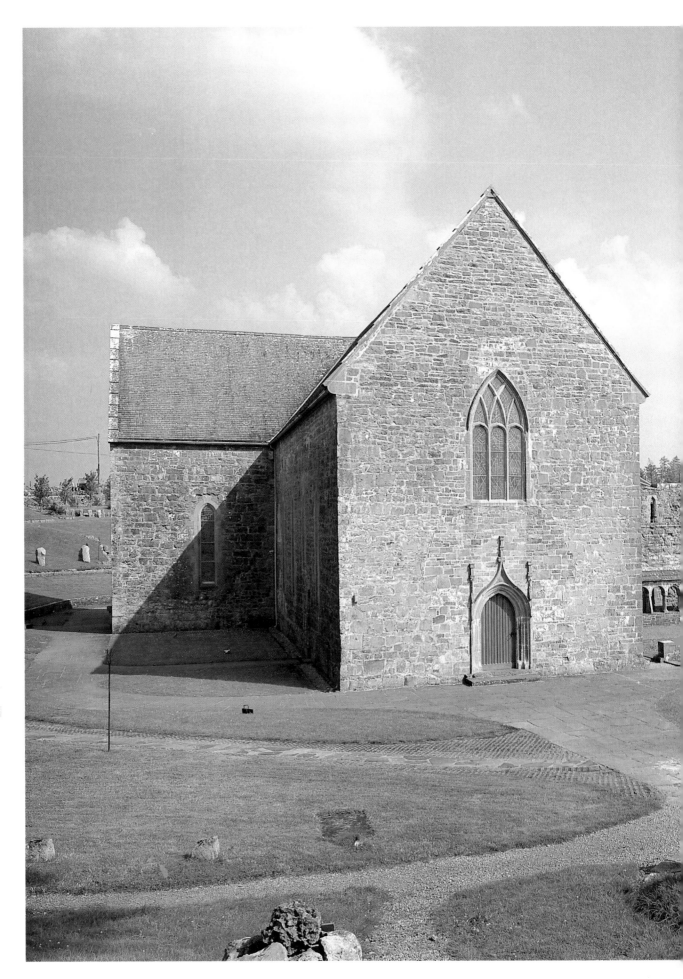

**Left** *Built of Mayo limestone, Ballintober Abbey was a royal foundation of the O Conor kings of Connacht for the Canons Regular of St Augustine in 1216. Its importance lay in its location as a starting point for the annual pilgrimage to the holy mountain of Croagh Patrick, some 15 miles (24km) to the west overlooking Clew Bay.*

**Below** *Cong Abbey, at the northern end of Lough Corrib, was also founded for the Augustinian canons by the O Conor kings of Connacht – but in the 12th century. The decorative stonework of the cloister arcade in the foreground was, however, carved in 1860 by Peter Foy, a stone carver in the employ of the local landlord, Sir Benjamin Lee Guinness.*

125

**Overleaf** *Kylemore Abbey is one of the classic beauty spots of Connemara. The wealthy Liverpool merchant, Mitchell Henry, MP (1826–1910), built the vast Victorian pile to serve as his home and his castle – civilisation in the midst of the Connemara wilderness, as it were. It is now a Benedictine convent of the Irish Dames of Ypres, who run a school here and provide refreshments for visitors.*

**Previous spread, left** *The traveller in Connemara is never far from a view of the mountains known as the Twelve Pins or Bens. (Gaelic beann, like Scottish Ben means a head or hilltop.) Even for the numerate, counting their exact number is said to cause considerable confusion – 11 or 13 being the usual count!*

**Previous spread, right**
*'Where the wandering water gushes from the hills above Glen-Car' wrote the poet WB Yeats about this entrancing spot in Co Sligo,
'there is a waterfall upon Ben Bulben side, that all my childhood counted dear;
were I to travel far and wide I could not find a thing so dear.'*

**Left** *Strong colours and straight lines make an interesting composition in the village-scape of Cong in Co Mayo.*

**Bottom left** *The small, traditional, family-owned shop of the Irish country town – as here at Castlerea, Co Roscommon – only rarely closes its doors to visitors during trading hours. It can't afford to do so, with so much competition coming from the larger and more impersonal supermarkets.*

**Above** *The Bridge Mill complex close to O'Brien's bridge is not just a pretty picture beside the River Corrib in Galway city. It is also a vibrant shopping venue, with restaurants, and arts and crafts of various sorts for sale.*

**Left** *The town of Clifden is justifiably called 'the capital of Connemara'. Unlike most Irish towns which just 'growed and growed', it was actually founded – by one John Darcy in 1812, and plays host to the colourful Connemara Pony Show in mid-August.*

133

**Left** *Clifden nestles at the top of the bay of the same name. But it has an uneasy relationship to its water frontage, as the main street runs slightly inland from the sea.*

**Left** *Of Co Mayo's two largest lakes, Lough Conn is the more northerly. While dominated to the west by the tall cone of Mount Nephin, its surroundings are otherwise low-lying, providing bathing and fishing facilities for those in search of contentment around its shores.*

**Below** *Dog's Bay is probably the finest of all the beaches of Connemara, ideal for the family paddle in summer. Its sand dunes have recently produced some of the area's earliest traces of human activity, dating from the Stone Age.*

135

136

**Right** *The Sky Road, west of Clifden, gets its name because it is 'as high as the sky', offering splendid views over the Atlantic Ocean.*

**Left** *Lough Key, in Co Roscommon, is the most beautifully wooded of all the lakes through which the River Shannon flows in the 214 miles (344km) of its length. The Rockingham Forest Park on its shore, near Boyle, provides the visitor with pleasant boating facilities.*

**Below** *Clew Bay is a gentle Atlantic inlet on the west coast of Co Mayo. Being a seascape of drowned drumlins, its myriad islands look like a shoal of whales. The bay is flanked on either side by hills, the most famous of which is Croagh Patrick.*

**Right** *One-sixth of Ireland's surface is covered by bog. Much of it is found in the flatter terrain of the midland counties, such as Roscommon. Rather than presenting a monotonous brown face, the bogs can beguile the botanist with an attractive and colourful range of flora. More recently, however, after massive exploitation for domestic fuel and gardeners' peat, they are now in need of preservation.*

**Above** *Coole Park, near Gort in Co Galway, was the home of Augusta, Lady Gregory (1852–1932), who, with the poet WB Yeats, spearheaded the Irish dramatic movement in the early years of this century. Her house is, sadly, no more, but in her garden is a copper beech tree on which many of her guests carved their initials – prominent among them the flourish of G(eorge) B(ernard) S(haw).*

141

**Left** *Westport House in Co
Mayo is the finest classical
house in the west of Ireland.
Located at the top of Clew
Bay, it is the home of Lord
Altamont, whose family, the
Marquesses of Sligo, have
lived here for more than 250
years. The house was
designed by Richard Cassels
around 1730, but additions
were made to it in 1778,
probably by Thomas Ivory.*

**Above** *The ornamental waters
in the grounds of Westport
House were achieved by
controlling the tides of an inlet
of Clew Bay. They offer safe
boating for those who visit the
numerous entertainment
facilities in the grounds.*

142

143

**Left** *Ashford Castle, at the northern (Mayo) end of Lough Corrib, started its life as a hunting lodge. Later converted into the style of a French château, it was given its present castle appearance by the Dublin brewer, Arthur Guinness, 1st and last Lord Ardilaun, who took his title from an island in the nearby lake. The castle is now a luxury hotel, which has numbered among its guests Ronald Reagan, former President of the United States of America.*

**Above left** *Clonalis House, near Castlerea in Co Roscommon, is a mansion of 1878–80 and the home of descendants of the O Conor Kings of Connacht, two of whom were High Kings of Ireland in the 12th century. In the grounds is their traditional inauguration stone. Inside, the house (open to the public) contains old family treasures, including costumes and uniforms, as well as a harp of the famous blind harpist of the 18th century, Turlough O'Carolan, who numbered the O Conors among his patrons.*

**Above** *Lissadell House, Co Sligo, is the home of the Gore-Booth family. (It is open to the public.) WB Yeats made it famous in his description of two daughters of the house,*
*'The light of evening, Lissadell,*
*Great windows open to the south,*
*Two girls in silk kimonos, both*
*Beautiful, one a gazelle.'*

**Overleaf** *The table mountain of Ben Bulben dominates the landscape of north Co Sligo, changing its shape wondrously depending on the angle from which it is viewed. It features in the old Irish love tale of Diarmuid and Gráinne, of whom the former found his death upon its slopes. For the poet Yeats, who lies buried in its shadow, a small white stone on its southern side was the door to faeryland, 'where you can buy joy for a penny'.*

144

ULSTER

**Previous page** *For the motorist driving northwards from Belfast or from the harbour at Larne, Ballygalley is a gateway to the Glens of Antrim. Made accessible by a coastal road in the 1830s, the Glens are one of Ulster's most spectacular touring landscapes, with views across to Scotland, which seems just a stone's throw away.*

**Left** *Not a fairy-tale castle on the Rhine, but Glenveagh Castle on Lough Veagh in the heart of the Donegal Highlands. Though in the Republic, Donegal is counted among the nine counties of ancient Ulster – and Glenveagh is one of its most romantic showpieces.*

**Left** *Glenveagh Castle, built by the Adair family in 1870, forms the core of the 10,000-acre Glenveagh estate. In 1983 it came into State ownership, and is now a National Park. Visitors leave their cars at the Interpretative Centre near the road and walk, or are brought by bus, to the castle, where guided tours are provided.*

**Below** *The gardens attached to Glenveagh Castle are a joy to behold. They were laid out in the last century by Cornelia Adair, wife of the first owner. In a comparatively short time, she managed to transform a barren boggy hillside into one of Ireland's foremost gardens, with a rich variety of rare and delicate plants. Her work was further enhanced by Henry McIlhenny, the last private owner, who lived at Glenveagh from 1937 until 1983.*

149

**Right** *A sun-dial forms a focal point in the beautifully tended garden of The Argory in Co Armagh. The house was built in 1824 on the banks of the River Blackwater for Walter McGeough, whose great grandson gave it to the National Trust in 1979. It has no electricity, the house having been lit by oxy-acetylene gas, made by its own plant which is still preserved in the courtyard.*

153

**Left** *The rope bridge at Carrick-a-Rede, near Ballintoy in Co Antrim, links the mainland to an island noted for its salmon fishery. Providing an exciting walk for the adventurous at heart, the bridge is removed during the winter months for reasons of safety.*

**Above** *Glenarm Bay is at the mouth of one of the Glens of Antrim, where woods and waterfalls intermingle in the shadow of great basalt cliffs. In the 5th century, the Glens formed the small kingdom of Dal Riada, which gained control of south-western Scotland, thereby paving the way for the creation of the kingdom of Scotland.*

**Right** *Horses graze in the bucolic surroundings of Grey Abbey in Co Down. This gently rolling countryside at the eastern end of the county is typical of the Ards Peninsula, a 15-mile-long (24km) tongue of land stretching southwards between Strangford Lough and the Irish Sea.*

**Left** *In the southern part of Co Down, the Mountains of Mourne sweep down to the sea, as Percy French says in his song. Inland, they enclose peaceful pastures along the valley floors.*

**Above** *The granite walls which add such forceful character to the Mourne landscape are often built of large boulders which create an impression that only a race of giants could have moved them into position. Yet the 'famine walls', climbing mindlessly over the hills, were built by hungry peasants in return for food during the appalling potato blight years of the 1840s.*

**Left** *Thatch is a material with which the Irish have roofed their buildings for centuries. The art of thatching declined earlier in this century, but is now undergoing a revival. In these tea-rooms at Bellanaleck in Co Fermanagh, thatch creates a feeling of character and cosiness.*

**Above** *This small window allows for the passing in and out of turf, or peat, in an old white-washed cottage at Dunlewy, in Co Donegal. Living at the foot of Mount Errigal, the village community at Dunlewy have recently restored the old farmhouse where Manus Ferry and his sister Sophie used to dye and weave their tweeds in the shadow of the Poisoned Glen.*

**Overleaf** *An interior view of the house from Lismacloskey, near Toome in Co Antrim, which is now reconstructed in the Ulster Folk and Transport Museum at Cultra, Co Down (see page 160). The house was built by a planter family in the 17th century, and served as a rectory in 1714. The furnishings, though not belonging to the house originally, re-create the life-style of an affluent family in rural Ulster around the turn of the century.*

**Above** *This house originally stood in Lismacloskey, near Toome in Co Antrim. After the Ulster Folk Museum was founded in 1958, the house was one of many from various locations in Ulster which were taken down stone by stone and re-assembled in the museum's grounds at Cultra, some seven miles (11km) from Belfast city centre.*

**Right** *Hannah Simpson, who lived in this house at Dergenagh, some three miles (5km) east of Ballygawley, Co Tyrone, was the mother of Ulysses Simpson Grant, the 18th President of the United States of America (1869–77). In the course of restoration work on the old homestead some years ago, parts of the house were found to go back to the early 17th century, when the Simpsons came from Scotland to settle here before emigrating again to the United States in the 19th century.*

**Above** *High-quality modern masonry helps to re-create an early Christian monastery, complete with round tower and stone church, in the Ulster History Park in Gortin Glen, near Omagh, Co Tyrone. The park brings vividly to life the living patterns in Ulster from the Stone Age to the Middle Ages.*

**Left** *The Ulster-American Folk Park at Camphill, near Omagh in Co Tyrone, re-creates the two vastly different worlds of the Ulster-Irish during the last few centuries. The houses they lived in before many of them left Ireland are contrasted with the houses, like this one, which they built on reaching the New World. A life-size reproduction of a ship of the period brings to life the atmosphere of the emigrant voyage, and forms a symbolic bridge uniting the two sides of the Atlantic Ocean.*

*163*

**Left** *First impressions are of a menacing totem better avoided on a dark night. But closer inspection of this stone statue in the old graveyard on Boa Island, Co Fermanagh, reveals that it consists of two human figures placed back to back. Usually taken to be some pagan Celtic two-faced god akin to the Roman Janus, it is now interpreted by some as an early Christian sculpture, the purpose of which remains as inscrutable as the faces themselves.*

**Above** *The peaceful ruined church of Grey Abbey in Co Down reveals one of the earliest examples of pure Gothic architecture in Ireland. The abbey was founded for the Cistercians in 1193 by Affreca, a native of the Isle of Man and wife of the county's Norman conqueror, John de Courcy. A stone effigy in the church may preserve her likeness, and could have been placed over her tomb.*

**Left** *The present cathedral at Downpatrick in Co Down retains the core of its 13th-century predecessor. Close by is a stone of c1900 which is said to mark the grave of Ireland's 5th-century national apostle, St Patrick. Although his name is closely linked with the town, there is no clear evidence that the saint was buried here. However, he probably did found a monastery at Downpatrick.*

165

**Above** *Powerful, yet enigmatic, faces emerge from two stone figures on White Island in Lough Erne. Dating from the 8th or 9th century, the figures have defied satisfactory explanation. They may have borne steps up to a pulpit or have carried a shrine containing the relics of some early Irish saint – perhaps those of St Molaise, who founded the monastery on another island in this beautiful Fermanagh lake.*

166

**Right** *Mussenden Temple, breathtakingly sited on a sea-cliff near Castlerock, six miles (9½km) from Coleraine, gets its name from a Mrs Frideswide Mussenden. It was built for her around 1783 as a summer-house library by her eccentric cousin, Frederick Hervey, the Earl-Bishop of Derry (1730–1803). It stands in the grounds of his estate at Downhill and is now owned by the National Trust.*

167

**Above left** *Dundrum is the mightiest of all the castles which protected the coast of Co Down during the Middle Ages. The walls, enclosing a massive round donjon or circular tower, were probably built by John de Courcy in the late 12th century to defend the lands which he had seized in the county. They proved no match for King John, who took the castle in 1210.*

**Above top** *The town of Carrickfergus, on the northern shore of Belfast Lough, is dominated by the best preserved of all the early Norman castles in Ireland. It, too, was probably constructed by John de Courcy after his initial conquest of Ulster in 1177, and was also taken by King John in 1210. The castle was considerably expanded during the 13th century, and it welcomed King William of Orange when he landed in Ireland in 1690.*

**Above** *Situated between Newry and Warrenpoint in Co Down, Narrow Water Castle stands romantically on a small promontory guarding the access to the Newry River from Carlingford Lough. The tower-house was built by John Sancky around 1560, but the battlemented bawn-wall enclosing it was heavily restored in the 19th century.*

**Left and above** *The 16th-century castle overlooking Strangford harbour in Co Down stood sentinel at one side of the entrance to Strangford Lough – matched on the other side by the castle at Portaferry. Strangford was already active in overseas trading in the 13th century, and 500 years later it was ranked as the eighth most important port in Ireland.*

**Left** *Annalong is a small and colourful port in Co Down. Its dock, cut out of the rock, was the only one along 12 miles (19km) of coast, and admirably served its small fishing community. It was also actively involved in the export of granite from the Mourne Mountains which form its hinterland. The mill beside the harbour probably dates from the early 19th century.*

**Above** *The area around Gortahork, in the north-western corner of Donegal, has an interesting collection of thatched houses, and one of Ireland's most extensive sand dunes. Students flock here to learn Irish, as it is one of the most important centres of the Donegal Gaeltacht, or region where Irish is the everyday language. It is also the best starting point for the climb to Muckish Mountain.*

**Right** *The Giant's Causeway, a World Heritage Site and National Nature Reserve, is Ireland's most famous natural phenomenon. Some 60 million years ago, great quantities of basalt cooled here into about 40,000 polygonal columns, creating spectacular formations with colourful modern names such as The Giant's Organ. Together with 10 miles (16km) of coastal walks, the Causeway is a property of the National Trust, which offers interpretative displays and tea-rooms at the entrance.*

**Below** *The climber who reaches the top of the gentle cone of Mount Errigal (2466 ft/752 m) is rewarded with a wonderful panorama. Dunlewy, with its 19th-century marble church, lies at the foot of the mountain, the highest in Donegal.*

174

**Previous page** *Mount Stewart House in Co Down, now a property of the National Trust, has one of the most outstanding gardens in these islands. Italianate in style, they are largely a creation of Edith, wife of the 7th Marquess of Londonderry. The house is an 1820s enlargement by William Vitruvius Morrison of an 1803–6 mansion built by the 1st Marquess, father of Viscount Castlereagh of Council of Vienna fame.*

**Above** *Florence Court lies snugly surrounded by wooded hills in south-west Fermanagh. The central block of the house, noted for its riot of baroque stucco work, was probably started early in the 18th century by Sir John Cole, who named it for his wife Florence Wrey of Cornwall. The wings were added some 50 years later.*

177

**Above and left** *In 1762,
Lady Ward and her husband,
Bernard (later Viscount
Bangor), could not agree on
the type of house they wished
to build at Castleward,
overlooking Strangford Lough
in Co Down. He wanted a
classical frontage, while she
wanted a façade in the latest
'Gothick style'. So the pair
reached an amicable
compromise – the house was
built with one face classical
(*left*) and the other Gothick –
but her side has the best view!
The walled garden (*above*)
plays host to many species of
indigenous birds. Castleward
now belongs to the National
Trust.*

**Right and below** *The
Annesley family took more
than a century to start
building their castle on the
estate which they had bought
at Castlewellan, Co Down, in
1741. It was the young 4th
Earl Annesley who finally
achieved the feat, and the
location he chose beside the
lake is more splendid than the
castle itself. The building was
completed in 1858 to a design
by William Burn. Sold to the
Government around 1965,
Castlewellan is now a Forest
Park, well known for its
gardens and arboretum.*

**Right** *Francis Johnston, a native of Armagh, was the architect of the city's Observatory. Building work commenced in 1789, the year of the French Revolution. A more recent appendage is the Planetarium of 1968 where Patrick Moore, the famous TV astronomer, presided as the first director. Inside, the audience can choose the pictures which are projected on to the dome of the building.*

**Below** *Located on one of the hills of Armagh, the Catholic cathedral was started in 1840 to designs by Thomas Duff of Newry. It was later altered to the existing twin-spired edifice by the noted Victorian architect, J J MacCarthy. On another of the city's hills stands the less lofty Protestant cathedral, which occupies the presumed site of St Patrick's own episcopal foundation of 444–5.*

**Right** *The Belleek Pottery Visitors' Centre on the banks of Lough Erne in Co Fermanagh offers an audio-visual theatre, a museum and a guided tour of the pottery. Feldspar from nearby Castle Cauldwell provides the basis for the translucent parian china, worked into delicate basketry and other forms, which has made the pottery's products internationally famous.*

**Above left and left** *Founded in 1608, Bushmills in Co Antrim is the world's oldest – and Ulster's only – licensed whiskey distillery. Each of its three splendid brands has a distinctive flavour, all matured in great rows of oak casks. When you taste them, you can readily understand the claim of the Russian Tsar Peter the Great, that 'of all wines the Irish spirit is the best'.*

**Above** *The massive Parliament Buildings at Stormont occupy a commanding site on the outskirts of Belfast. A gift from the British Government, the neo-classical building was designed by the Liverpool architect Arnold Thornley and completed in 1932, when the official opening ceremony was performed by King George V.*

**Right** *A jester (not unsuitably) overlooks the entrance to the Grand Opera House in Belfast's Great Victoria Street. One of the city's more baroque structures, the Opera House was the creation of Frank Matcham of London and was built in 1894–5. It was sympathetically restored between 1976 and 1980, and is one of the cultural jewels in the crown of Ulster's capital city.*

185

**Above** *Ferns, bamboos and palms luxuriate in the Tropical Ravine House in Belfast's Botanic Gardens. Built in 1886–9, doubled in length between 1900 and 1902, and re-roofed in 1980, the Ravine gets its name from the man-made sunken glen within, which is viewed from a balcony-walk around the perimeter.*

**Left** *Belfast's great City Hall in Donegall Square glows in the evening light. Designed by A B Thomas of London, it represents one of the finest examples of the Baroque Revival style in the British Isles, its floodlit dome echoing St Paul's Cathedral and Greenwich Hospital. The building exudes the city's pride in its prosperity around the turn of the century.*

*187*

**Overleaf** *. . . And as the sun sets over beautiful Tranarossan Bay on the rocky Donegal coastline, we come to the end of this journey through Ireland in pictures.*

188

# INDEX

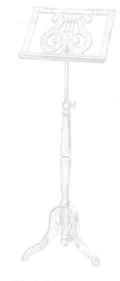

# ACKNOWLEDGEMENTS

*L BLAKE* 70/1 Powerscourt, 77 Kilbeggan – Lock's Distillery, 81 Wexford Heritage Park, 85 Dublin Pub, 87 Georgian Door, 102/3 Trinity College, Dublin, 114/5 Rosses Point, 116/7 Eyre Square Dublin, 117 Knock, 118/9 Ballina, 119 Salthill funfair, 120 Connemara's Sky Drive, 120/1 Roundstone, 122 Boyles Abbey, 124/5 Ballintober Abbey, 125 Royal Abbey of Cong, 126/7 Kylemore Abbey, 128 Twelve Pins, 129 Glencar Waterfall, 130 Castlerea shopfront, 131 Galway Bridge Mill Complex, 132/3 Clifden, 133 Clifden, 134/5 Lough Conn, 135 Dog's Bay, 136/7 Lough Key, 137 Connemara, Clew Bay, 138/9 Bogland, 140/1 Westport House, 141 Westport House, 142/3 Castlerea, Clonalis House, 143 Lissadell House, 143 Cong, Ashford Castle, 144/5 Ben Bulben Mountain.

*J BLANDFORD* 8/9 Moll's Gap, 10/11 The Vee, Drombeg Stone Circle, 11 Glenfahan, Dunbeg, 15 Mizen Head Lighthouse, 16 Flora, 18/9 St Finbarr's Hermitage, 19 Killarney Cathedral, 20 Baltimore Harbour, 21 Glandore Harbour, 21 Baltimore Harbour, 24/5 Macroom, 25 Cork, Schull Village, 27 Anascaul, Dingle Pub, 27 Pub in Macroom, 28/9 Muckross House, 28 Killarney, 29 Molls Gap, 30 Jarveys & Trap, 30/1 Ladies View, Killarney, 32 Gougane Barra, 32/3 Connor Pass, 34 Towards Allihies, Donkey, 34/5 Coumeenoole, 36 Blarney Stone, 36/7 Blarney Castle, 38 Kanturk Castle, 39 Lismore Castle, 40/1 Sneem, 41 Ross Carbery, 42 Dunmanus Bay, 43 Glengarriff Harbour, 43 Towards Crookhaven, 44/5 Schull Harbour, 46/7 Ring of Kerry, 48/9 Italian Gardens, 48 Bantry House, 52/3 Mountain Views Kenmare & Glengarriff, Healy Pass, Nr Caherciveen, 54 Baltimore Bay, Inch Strand, 55 Cliffs of Moher, Waterville Kerry, 56/7 Mitchelstown Caves, 58/9 Dunquin Harbour, 60/1 Bog village recreation, 62/3 Great Blasket Island, 64/5 Nr Fahan.

*D FORSS* 12/3 Kilmallock, 12 Timoleague Abbey, 14 Youghal Beach, 15 Old Head of Kinsale, 16/7 Lough Gur, 22/3 Cobh, 26 Kinsale, 41 Signpost, 44 Kinsale, 57 Nr Courtmacsherry Bay, 63 Lough Gur, 74/5 Monasterboice, 80 The Mill Ballytore, 82/3 Powerscourt House, O'Connell St, 84 Merrion Row, Foley's Pub, James Joyce Statue, 88/9 Christ Church cathedral, 95 Japanese Gardens, Kildare, 108/9 Dublin O'Connell St, 109 Plaque, Dublin, 123 Turoe stone Loughrea, 130 Cong, 139 Autograph Tree, Coole Park, 146/7 Ballygalley, 152/3 Glenarm, 154 Nr Greyabbey, 162 Greyabbey, 167 Carrickfergus Castle, 168/9 Strangford Harbour.

*T KING* 74/5 Glendalough, 99 Skerries, 108/9 O'Connoll Monument Dublin.

*G MUNDAY* 148/9 Glenveagh Lough and Castle, 149 Glenveagh Castle, Gardens, 154/5 Mourne Mountains, 157 Cottage, Dunlewy, 160 Lismacloskey House, Ulysses Grant Homestead, 161 Irish History Park, 164/5 Downpatrick Cathedral, 166 Narrow Water Castle, 172/3 Giants Causeway, 174/5 Mount Stewart House, 177 Castleward Gardens and House, 178/9 Castlewellan Lake, Castle, Gardens, 180/1 Armagh 181 St Patrick's Cathedral Armagh, 182/3 Belleek Pottery, 184/5 Belfast, Stormont, Grand Opera House, Botanic Gardens, 186/7 Belfast City Hall.

*THE SLIDE FILE* 70 Avondale House, 72 Newgrange, 75 Sheepgate and Town Walls, 76/7 Guinness Brewery, 78/9 Marley Park Bookbinder, 79 Rathborne's Candlemaker, Harp Maker, 81 Silk Painting, 85 Fiddlers, 86 Abbey Theatre Posters, Dublin, Fitzwilliam Square Doorway, Georgian Door Knocker, 89 St Michael's Church carvings, 90/1 Dublin Castle, 93 Chester Beatty Library, Belvedere House, 94 Palm House, Dublin, 95 Powerscourt Demesne, 96/7 Royal Dublin Society, 96 Phoenix Park Zoo, 97 Phoenix Park Zoo, 98 Balbriggan, 100/1 Slane River, 102 Thomas Burgh's Library, 104 National Gallery Dublin, 105 Trinity College Chapel, St Anne's Church, 106/7 Fitzwilliam Square, 107 Ely House, Olympia Theatre, 109 Horse and cart, 110/1 Malahide Castle, Frieze Sunlight Chambers, 113 Stoneheads Iveagh Market.

*P ZOELLER* 13 Rock of Cashel, 23 Mill Town Malby, 32 Farmlands, 38 Nenagh Castle, Waterford, 49 Adare House, 50/1 Carrick on Suir, Limerick King John's Castle, 51 Bunratty Castle, Glin Castle, 66/7 Thatched Windmill Tacumashane, 74 Kells, 82 Wexford, 92/3 Abbeyleix House and Gardens, 99 Courtown Harbour.